IMAGES
of America

EL DORADO
LEGACY OF AN OIL BOOM

IMAGES
of America

EL DORADO
LEGACY OF AN OIL BOOM

Jay M. Price

ARCADIA
PUBLISHING

Published by Arcadia Publishing
Charleston, South Carolina

Library of Congress Catalog Card Number: 2005931501

For all general information contact Arcadia Publishing at:
Telephone 843-853-2070
Fax 843-853-0044
E-mail sales@arcadiapublishing.com
For customer service and orders:
Toll-Free 1-888-313-2665

Visit us on the Internet at www.arcadiapublishing.com

CONTENTS

Acknowledgments   6

Introduction   7

1.   Black Gold   9

2.   Oil Dorado   27

3.   The Business of Oil   45

4.   Oil As a Way of Life   75

5.   The Legacy Continues   101

Bibliography   128

ACKNOWLEDGMENTS

Books of this type are always team efforts. I am very appreciative for all the assistance that I received from the staff of the Kansas Oil Museum; Wichita State University Libraries, Department of Special Collections; the Wichita-Sedgwick County Historical Museum; the Kansas Aviation Museum; Kansas Geological Society; Augusta Historical Museum; Douglass Pioneer Museum; Kansas Oil and Gas Hall of Fame and Museum; Kansas Independent Oil and Gas Association (KIOGA); and the Wichita Public Library. Many individuals have been valuable sources and sounding boards. These include Brad and Deborah Amend, William Bischoff, Robert Cowdery, Roxie Olmstead, John Gries, Craig Miner, Lee Phillips, Day Radebaugh, Tom Tatlock, Marvin Frankamp, Dudley Toevs, and Cliff Stone. Finally, I want to say thank you to the many friends, family, colleagues, and students who have all been supportive and valuable sounding boards for this project. Thanks also go to all the photographers, professional and amateur, who took the images that went into this book. Unless otherwise noted, all photographs come from the collections at the Kansas Oil Museum in El Dorado.

INTRODUCTION

Dramatic mining booms such as the California gold rush, the Comstock Lode, and the Klondike were exciting parts of the history of the United States. In each place, a mineral resource seemed to promise instant wealth for any willing to take advantage of the opportunities. Thousands arrived, often building whole communities nearly overnight. Yet it took resources to harness resources—and considerable risk. Investment in equipment and workers often resulted in more frustration than fortune. Success usually came to persons and companies that already had established track records and experience. "Rags to riches" was the exception not the rule.

The petroleum industry has experienced similar booms, one of which was in Butler County, Kansas, from the second decade of the 20th century through the 1920s. A region that was known primarily for its agriculture became the location of one of the largest oil strikes of the time. The Allied Forces High Command recognized the need for oil during World War I and transformed what had once been the farm town of El Dorado into a petroleum center. The boom had a profound influence on the lives of people in El Dorado, Wichita, Augusta, Towanda, and beyond. Workers came in to find relatively well paying but hard work, moving into company towns such as Oil Hill and Midian. Teams of geologists searched for more deposits, in the process establishing the practices, training, and standards of their profession.

The oil industry in Butler County involved changes in technology and economics as much as personal drive, skill, and labor. When exploration began, wooden derricks housed cable tool rigs that literally pounded deep holes in the ground. Toward the end of the boom, the rotary drill was becoming standard. In economics, the automobile and airplane became widespread and the consumer replaced the military and heavy industry as the main outlet for oil products. That side of the oil industry, too, appeared in Butler County with names like Skelly, Vickers, and Phillips.

Like many booms, the one in El Dorado has had long-lasting impacts on the community well after the initial burst of activity. New opportunities in other parts of the state and region reshaped places like El Dorado and Augusta. Several oil communities and oil camps eventually disappeared. Even so, the exciting years of the boom live on in the pumps that still dot the landscape, the refinery work in El Dorado, and the memory preserved in institutions such as the Kansas Oil Museum.

Today, the hills and plains of south-central Kansas are quiet places. The loudest sounds come from the wind rustling through the grasses, punctuated by the occasional mooing cow and birdcall. About a century ago, however, the scene was very different as crews ventured out to construct wooden rigs and pound deep holes in the ground, searching for oil. Rigs, tanks, pipes, and even whole communities sprouted up nearly overnight in the early years of the 20th century. As the decades passed, the search for petroleum moved to other parts of the state, and quiet returned to the land. Today, however, as demand for oil reaches global proportions, there is talk that the crews may be back again. (Author's collection.)

One

BLACK GOLD

Desire for gold drew Spanish explorers into the interior of the Americas. In their ears rang stories of the wealth of the Incas, a legendary gilded king named El Dorado, and even whole cities made of gold. Francisco Vasquez de Coronado ventured out on to the plains in search of this very metal but returned disappointed. Centuries later, American farmers concluded that there was indeed gold on the plains, but it grew in the form of crops or as grasses that fed cattle. Others concluded that the real wealth of the region lay under the ground in the form of petroleum or what they sometimes called rock oil. This "black gold" promised riches for those willing to get it, transforming Kansas, especially that region near the southern edge of the Flint Hills between El Dorado and Wichita.

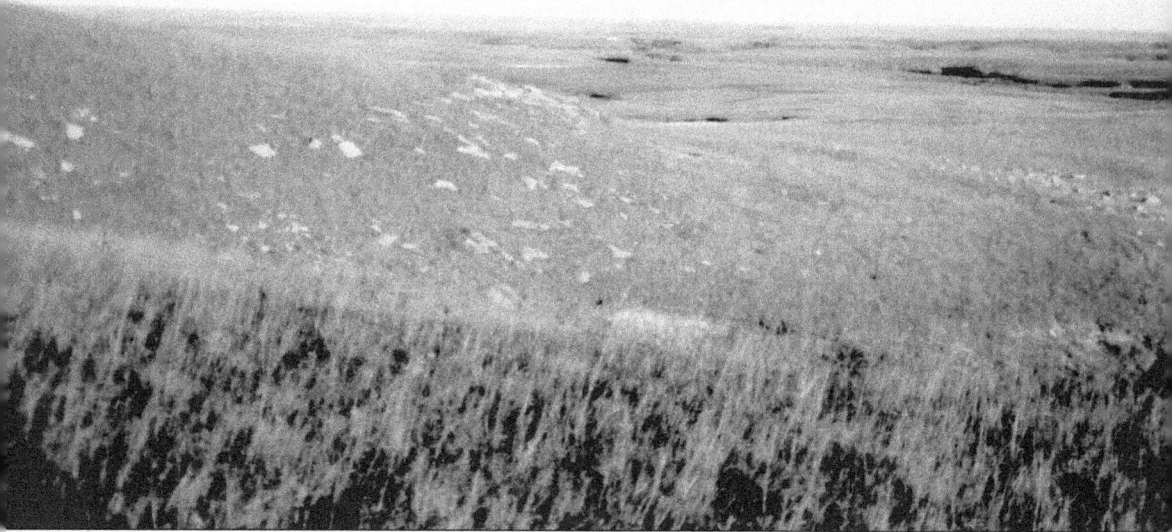

Beneath the grasses of the Great Plains, rock formations held pockets of oil and natural gas. Just as water flows underground through aquifers, oil oozes through porous stone. When a geologic feature blocks the flow of oil, pools form, often with pockets of natural gas and water above the oil itself. In Kansas, the Nemaha Ridge has allowed pools to form along its eastern edge. Pools stretched from the east and the south and extended into what is today southeastern Kansas and northeastern Oklahoma. (Author's collection.)

Sometimes pools of oil pitch, or bitumen, oozed to the surface. Native Americans, like most peoples before the 1800s, found only limited uses for the material. Bitumen could be used to make things watertight. It also had lighting and medicinal uses. (Courtesy Wichita State University Libraries, Department of Special Collections.)

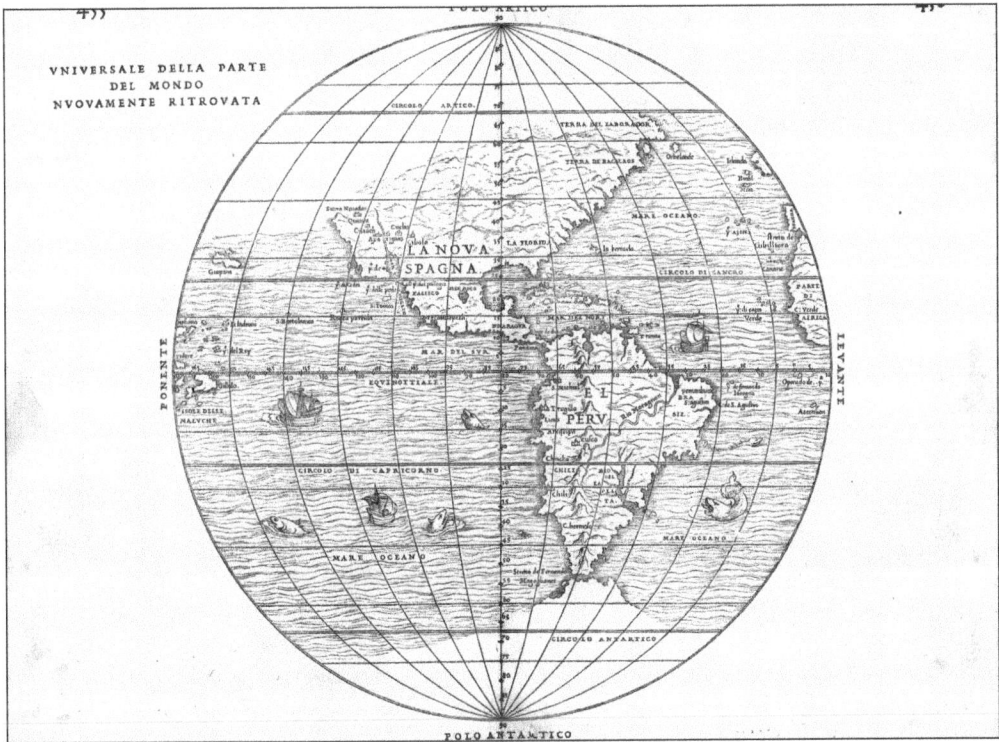

The first Europeans to venture into the region were the Spanish under Francisco Vasquez de Coronado. In 1541, he sought a place of great riches called Quivira, a place that he never found, even though it is listed in this 1550s map. Meanwhile, in South America, native peoples told the Spanish of a king named El Dorado. Covered with powered gold, this gilded man performed rituals with golden implements. (Courtesy Wichita State University Libraries, Department of Special Collections.)

By the 1800s, settlers and traders entered the area building cabins such as the Connor Cabin, now preserved at the Kansas Oil Museum. One settler found the place so beautiful that he supposedly exclaimed excitedly, "El Dorado!" The community that he helped develop along the banks of the Walnut River has kept that name ever since. For many years, the name was written as one word: Eldorado. (Author's collection.)

James R. Mead was one of the leading entrepreneurs in south-central Kansas. In the 1860s, he set up a trading post with the Osage and other tribes along the Whitewater River. The town of Towanda developed on the bluffs above "Mead's Ranche." (Courtesy Wichita State University Libraries, Department of Special Collections.)

The trading post of Augusta was named after the wife of one of the owners. During the early 1870s, Augusta challenged El Dorado as the county seat, one of many such county struggles in the decade. Resistance on the part of El Doradans, as well as the decision of the Kansas Supreme Court, confirmed the seat for El Dorado. (Courtesy Augusta Historical Society.)

Railroads were important tools in development, and towns developed along the lines of the Santa Fe and the Frisco. These towns included Andover, Potwin, Rosalia, and Beaumont, whose water tower, shown here, is still a local landmark. (Author's collection.)

In 1910, Butler County had a population of just over 23,000, of whom 3,100 lived in El Dorado, the county seat and largest town. The population had remained relatively steady since the 1880s. The courthouse at the top of the picture dates from 1909.

In June 1914, a tornado (called a cyclone then) hovered over El Dorado. In true Kansan fashion, the locals went out to look at it instead of heading for shelter.

14

Several years of dry weather and low corn prices encouraged Butler County farmers to grow a variety of sorghum called kafir (or kaffir) corn. By 1911, there were nearly 60,000 acres under cultivation. In October of that year, a fraternal organization called the Knights of Mapira established the first Kaffir Corn Festival to celebrate the plant. Different groups and communities sponsored booths and displays that lined the streets.

In the early 1900s, J. C. Robison constructed this massive barn northwest of Towanda as part of a complex to board and trade prize show horses. Eventually, Robison's Whitewater Falls Stock Farm advertised itself as "the largest Percheron breeding farm in the West." (Author's collection.)

A mixture of bluestem and short grasses were native to Butler County, but it was not until the late 1800s that Penrose Jackson proposed large-scale cattle raising in the county. Among these ranchers was Robert Hazlett, who became known for his Hereford cattle. Eventually, Hazlett's herd numbered 600 head.

Exploration for oil in Kansas began just before the outbreak of the Civil War. Tradition puts the first strikes in Miami County. In the decades that followed, exploration extended into southeastern Kansas. The 1890s saw a significant upsurge in exploration in the vicinity of Neodesha in Wilson County. A few years later, there were over 40 wells in the region.

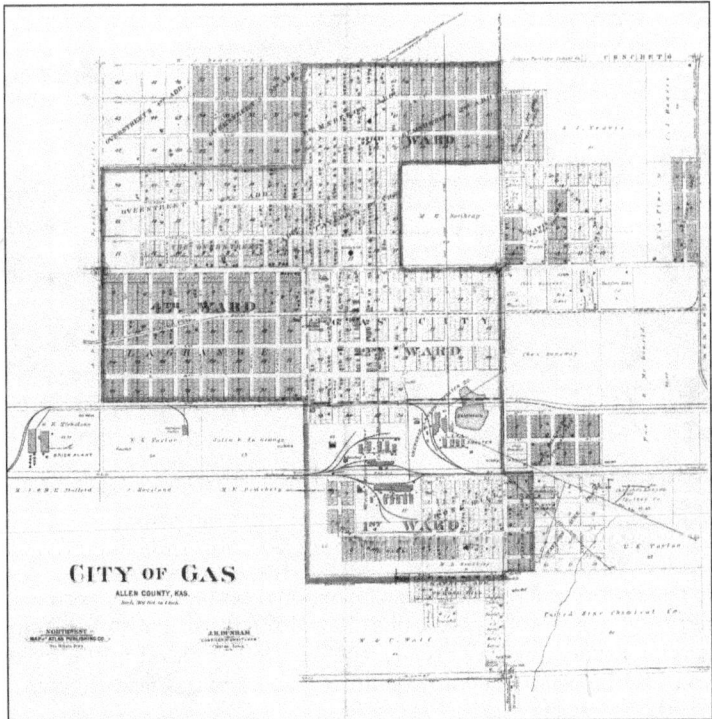

E. K. Taylor in Allen County developed a small community in 1898 after a well drilled there produced natural gas. Originally called Gas City, the town is now simply known as Gas. (Courtesy Wichita State University Libraries, Department of Special Collections.)

Standard Oil developed some of the earliest leases in Kansas. In the early 1900s, however, a number of Kansan oilmen and their sympathetic political supporters rallied against the John Rockefeller's Standard dominance. The movement encouraged Rockefeller to focus attention—and resources—on other parts of the country. However, in the second decade of the 20th century, other subsidiaries such as Carter Oil returned to Kansas to develop leases in the El Dorado field.

In the 19th century, Kansas was the regional center that supported activities in American Indian territory to the south. Then came oil. In 1897, the Cudahy Oil Company found oil at Bartlesville, and for a time, that city became the new center for oil in the region. As it turned out, Kansas and Oklahoma straddle a large array of oil and gas fields known as the Mid-Continent field. (Author's collection.)

The petroleum industry and the automobile industry reinforced each other. In the 19th century, oil had primarily industrial uses. In the 20th century, however, tractors, automobiles such as Henry Ford's Model T, and small engines created an unprecedented use of oil products among the general public.

Households and businesses once relied on gas manufactured in local plants. Society gradually learned that natural gas, which early oil drillers had burned off as a useless byproduct, was superior to manufactured gas as a household fuel. Even so, it took a while to convince America's housewives that "cooking with gas" was safe and convenient.

Founded by Henry Doherty, Cities Service became as a nationwide conglomerate of public utility companies, one of which was the Wichita Natural Gas Company. By the early 1900s, Cities Service expanded into the drilling, transporting, and storing of natural gas.

Cities Service's Wichita Natural Gas Company was based out of Bartlesville. The company started drilling test wells in Butler County but with little initial success. In the years that followed, however, Cities Service's extension company, Empire, helped develop the El Dorado field. The staff of Cities Service's Oil Hill office appears in this photograph.

In the early 1900s, a group of Augusta entrepreneurs formed the Augusta Oil, Gas, Mining and Prospecting Company and began drilling near that community. Initial test wells turned up natural gas but little oil. (Courtesy Augusta Historical Society.)

In March 1914, drilling crews hit oil on the farm of Frank Varner in Augusta. However, lack of transportation systems and demand precluded commercial drilling on the lease until late 1915. In October 1919, the Varner family poses in front of the oil wells on their farm for this photograph. (Author's collection.)

From 1909 to 1911, the city of El Dorado got into the drilling business when it sank two wells. Both were unsuccessful. Determined to find oil, El Dorado hired Erasmus Haworth, who was head of geology at Kansas University and the state geologist. In 1914, at his suggestion, the city of El Dorado drilled a well on the Fowler lease west of town in the middle of what would become the El Dorado field. Yet this test well, too, happened to turn up dry! Frustrated, the city turned over its 790 acres of leases to the Wichita Natural Gas Company for $800.

In the fall of 1915, Wichita Natural Gas started drilling on the lease of John Stapleton, an absentee owner living in Illinois, about five miles northwest of El Dorado. Wichita Natural Gas had Enos Ferguson, seen here standing next to his team, haul the first rig to the site. By the end of September, driller W. G. Obins and his crew were ready to start the process.

The crew anticipated going down about 3,000 feet, a process expected to take well over a month. October 7 is usually considered the day that the crew "struck oil" at about 550 feet down. It took four more months for drilling to reach its final depth of 2,465 feet.

Oil exploration attracted some interest but was not yet a great concern. In fact, the *Walnut Valley Times*'s major stories for October 1915 related to the war in Europe, the Kaffir Corn Festival, and the World Series. At first, those involved wanted to keep things quiet to prevent a rush of rivals. However, rumors that there was a major oil strike around El Dorado spread among those at the event, especially when arriving oil men started competing with festival attendees for accommodations in hotels such as the Metropolitan.

Metropolitan Hotel — Eldorado, Kans.

Meanwhile, Wichita Natural Gas discovered a gas flow outside of Beaumont, southeast of El Dorado on the Butler-Greenwood county line. The scene probably looked similar to this one.

By late October, the word was out. There was oil in Butler County that might rival fields in California and Oklahoma. Wichita Natural Gas made preparations for more drilling—as did a number of other speculators. A *Walnut Valley Times* article mused that "perhaps we'll have oil rigs in every yard after a while."

By 1917, developments expanded beyond the initial strike. The largest was the Towanda Pool to the west of El Dorado. Another major pool extended south from Augusta to Gordon with a further pool near Douglass. Some development took place in the east of the county at the line with Greenwood County. An additional area of exploration was in the county's northwestern corner. (Courtesy Wichita State University Libraries, Department of Special Collections.)

Two

OIL DORADO

El Dorado was at the northern end of the Mid-Continent field, a vast collection of oil pools that lay under eastern Oklahoma and southeastern Kansas. Although local businessmen were involved early on, branches of national firms conducted much of the major development. Empire Oil, a creation of Henry Doherty, Cities Service's founder, was the dominant company in the area, operating about three-fourths of the wells. The Carter Oil Company was a Standard Oil affiliate, while Gypsy was connected to Gulf Oil. Meanwhile, entrepreneurs such as Harry Sinclair, Archibald Derby, and William Skelly got their start in the already booming Oklahoma oil fields and sought new opportunities to the north. World War I and the needs of national defense launched this already booming scene into national prominence. By the end of the Great War, the fields between Wichita and El Dorado were among the most productive in the nation.

Within weeks of striking oil at Stapleton No. 1, representatives of oil companies in southeastern Kansas, Oklahoma, and elsewhere started flooding into El Dorado, looking for landowners willing to lease lands for oil exploration. Landowners knew a good deal when they saw one, and leases went from the usual $1 an acre in the early years of the second decade of the 20th century to scores and even hundreds of dollars almost overnight.

Archibald L. Derby grew up in the oil fields of Pennsylvania. Getting his start as a laborer on drilling crews, he worked his way up into the business. When the southeastern Kansas fields opened up, he came out to Independence and Chanute. When Oklahoma offered its opportunities, he took part in that boom as well. In early 1916, Derby and several others started drilling on the Wilson lease relatively close to Stapleton No. 1. Nobody was quite sure how large the field actually was; the farther away from Stapleton crews drilled, the riskier the initial investment. Derby's explorations paid off, and he went on to found the Derby Oil Company in 1920, which, a few years later, had a chain of service stations across four states and a refinery in Wichita.

A Scene In The Augusta Oil Fields.

Empire also expanded drilling in southern Butler County, initially concentrating on a field between Augusta and Gordon. In Augusta, "the crowds were so dense," according to newspaperman Rolla Clymer, "that at midnight it was difficult to walk down State Street."

Looking No. on Main St.   Augusta, Kans

(2) Trapshooter's Oil Well #2
© C. O. Boston. El Dorado Kans.

The Towanda area saw some of the most spectacular strikes on leases such as Trapshooters, Shumway, Ralston, Shriver, Boyer, and Enyart. For example, 11 hunting companions got together to drill for oil, forming a company called Trapshooters. The Trapshooters drilled on the Williams and Walker lease to the southwest of Stapleton in early 1917. They sold half the interest in the lease to the Eureka Oil and Gas Company of Kansas City to help finance the operation. In May of that year, just one month after the United States went to war, the drillers struck oil at 2,415 feet. This was one of the most productive wells in the field, producing between 10,000 and 15,000 barrels a day. The oil flowed so heavily that it temporarily overwhelmed the storage tanks. People came out from El Dorado on weekends just to look.

The Gypsy Oil Company, affiliated with the Gulf Pipe Line Company, began drilling for oil on the Shumway near Towanda, striking oil in July 1917. Within 10 months of the first strike, the Shumway produced $12 million worth of oil. By 1918, there were over 30 oil wells and 7 gas wells in the area.

Gypsy No. 5 on the Shumway became one of the most famous oil wells in the El Dorado field. The drilling crew struck oil in September 1917, and at a time when most wells produced under 25 barrels a day, this well started producing over 16,000 to 18,000 barrels a day—a record for the field. A total of two and a quarter million barrels flowed from the well for 222 days.

Although Standard Oil had been broken up in 1911, the various parts of the Standard empire were involved in the El Dorado field. For example, the Carter Oil Company was an affiliate of Standard Oil Company of New Jersey and had been very successful in exploring for oil in Oklahoma, becoming one of the largest producers in that state. By 1916, the Carter Oil Company looked to expand and concentrated its development efforts on the Porter lease, shown here.

The Phillips oil empire began with several brothers who came to Bartlesville in the early 1900s, becoming established in the banking and oil businesses. L. E. Phillips and Frank Phillips (shown here) had the most interest in oil exploration in Oklahoma and later, Kansas. In 1917, they consolidated their assets to form Phillips Petroleum. The company's activities centered on the Osage tracts by Bartlesville but extended into Cowley County and Butler County in Kansas.

In northern Butler County, near Elbing, drilling began on the Leydig farm in 1917, the Parris lease in 1918, and the Lathrop farm in 1919. Jack Vickers's success on the Parris lease led to other investments, including establishing a refinery at Potwin in 1920.

Oil development expanded to the southeast of El Dorado as well. Developments included Haverhill Petroleum's work on the Smock and Sluss pools. Later development included the Leon and Blankenship pools, mostly the work of Empire Oil and Gas.

This was an age of mechanized warfare, with gasoline-powered trucks, tanks, and aircraft. Naval technology was transitioning from coal to oil-burning engines. Machines of all types needed lubricants. Editor Rolla Clymer once said that "oceans" of oil "helped float the Allies to victory in both World Wars I and II." (Courtesy Wichita State University Libraries, Department of Special Collections.)

THE LIBERTY "PETROL"

GASOLINE
FOR THE ARMY

MACHINE
OIL

FUEL OIL
FOR THE ARMY

THE KAISER'S TRAIL

Courtesy The Wichita Eagle and Mr. B F. Hammond

During the early years of the boom, the United States was neutral in the European Great War. In April 1917, the United States entered the conflict, and the demand for oil mushroomed. In 1914, the price of crude oil was between 30¢ and 40¢ a barrel. By 1916, the price had gone to $1.55 and soon reached $3.50 a barrel.

Butler County sent more than just oil to the war effort. Women and men from Butler County were among the more than 83,000 Kansans who served during the Great War. Many served in the 35th, 42nd, and 89th Divisions. Over 10,000 served in the navy. This group of draftees is in front of the courthouse.

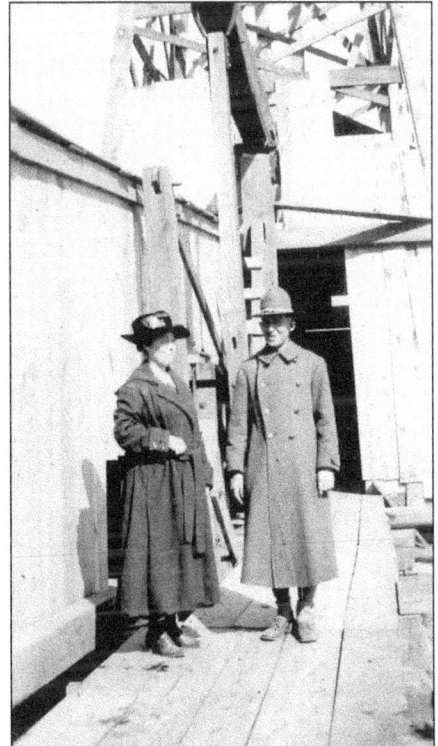

Harry Gilmore of El Dorado was one Kansan to serve in the Great War. Gilmore served with the 353rd Regiment of the 89th Division in France and participated the occupation of Germany. Meanwhile, his parents' farm, like many in the region, had an oil lease on it. In this photograph, he stands with his sister Carrie before going overseas to France. Gilmore survived the conflict, returning to El Dorado in 1919.

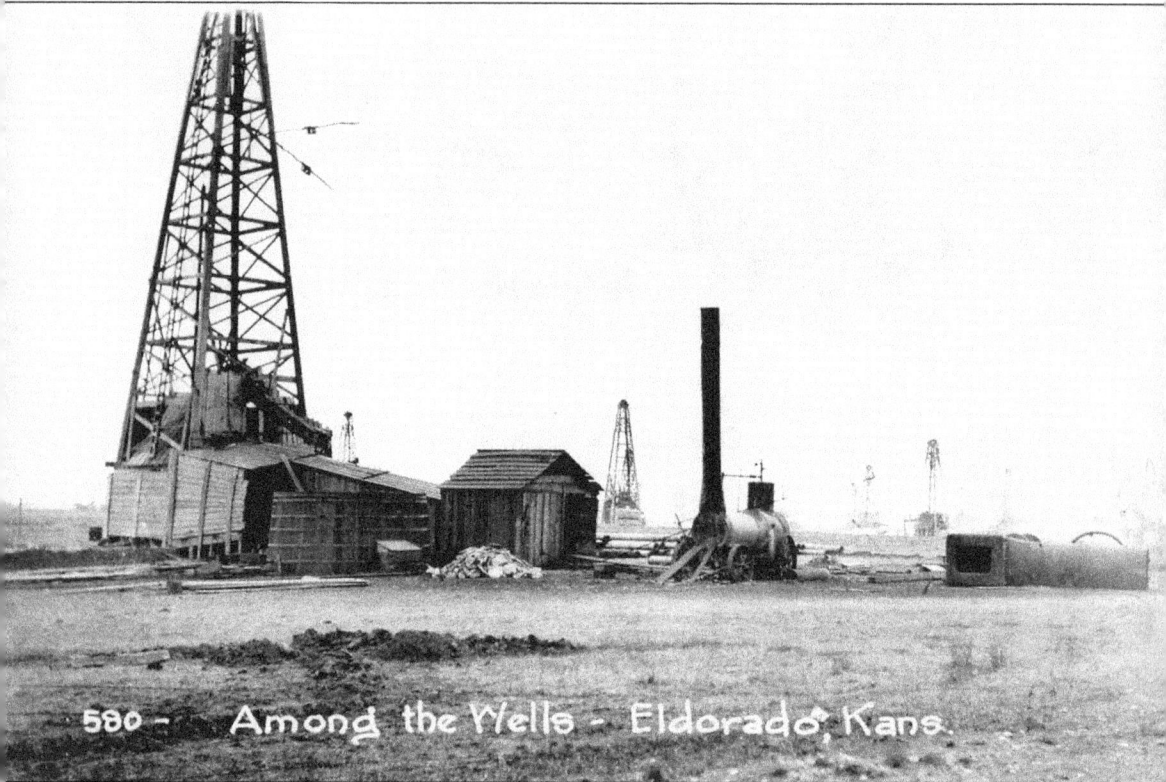

580 - Among the Wells - Eldorado, Kans.

In 1915, Kansas produced a modest 2.8 million barrels of oil. By 1917, Kansas produced over 36 million barrels of crude petroleum. In 1918, production peaked at over 45 million barrels. Kansas had become one of the leading oil states of the nation along with California (the leading producer), Oklahoma, and Texas.

After the war, oil production shifted to commercial use, and exploration expanded primarily to the south and east of the main El Dorado field. Exploration focused on a series of long, narrow fields called the "Shoestring Sands" in the southern and eastern parts of the county. The Derby Oil Company, for example, tapped several of these leases in southern Butler County during the 1920s. (Both images courtesy Wichita-Sedgwick County Historical Museum.)

John A. Vickers grew up in Liberal, Kansas, and initially went into the grain business. Seeing greater opportunities in petroleum, he moved to Butler County in 1918. He was active in both oil production and processing, founding Vickers Petroleum Company and Vickers Refining Company. He also developed Vickers Petroleum into one of the largest service station chains in the country.

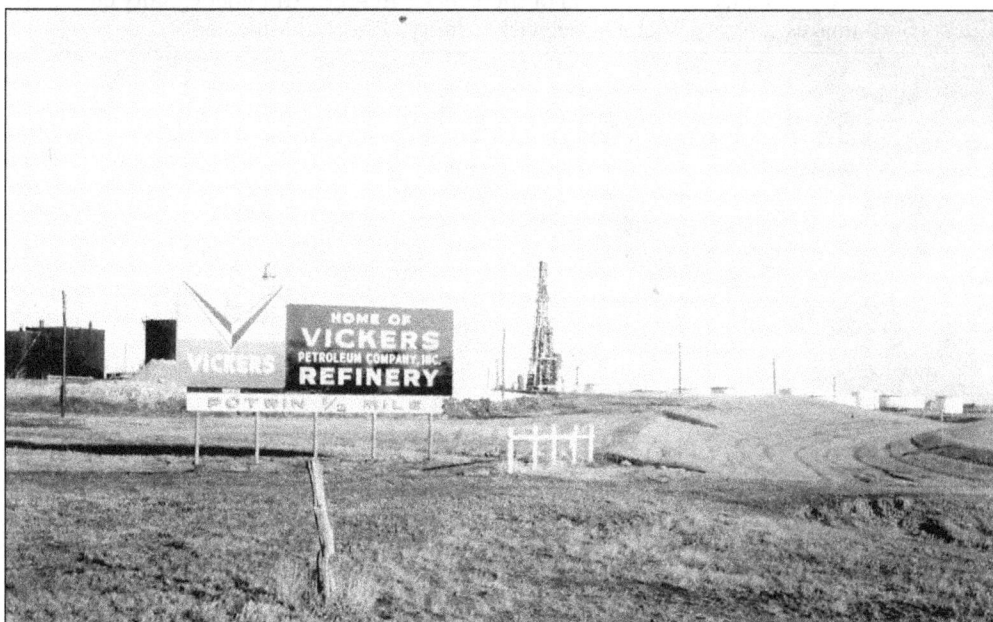

By 1918, there were eight refineries in the vicinity of El Dorado and Augusta. The White Eagle Refinery was in Augusta. The Vickers Refinery was in Potwin. El Dorado had two refineries: the El Dorado Refining Company, or "El Reco," to the north of town and what became the Skelly Refinery to the south. In the early 1920s, Derby built a refinery in Wichita as well. Several other, smaller refineries also developed but were often short lived.

William Grove Skelly grew up in Erie, Pennsylvania, and served in the Spanish-American War. By the second decade of the 20th century, Skelly had become one of the most successful oilmen in the Mid-Continent field. His Tulsa-based Skelly Oil Company expanded into the El Dorado field, establishing a refinery in El Dorado. Later on, the company set up a gasoline plant in Kingman County, the basis of a small community known as Skellyville.

Skelly's operations in El Dorado centered on two companies. One was the Midland Refining Company, formed in 1917 to operate a refinery in El Dorado. The other company was the Inland Oil Company, whose purpose was to drill oil for the refinery. In 1923, both firms merged with the recently founded Skelly Oil Company. Pete Simmons stands in the foreground of this photograph.

Born in West Virginia, Harry Ford Sinclair grew up in Independence, Kansas. He graduated from the University of Kansas's pharmacy school but made oil his career. He started by selling lumber for derricks and went on to establish a series of drilling, refining, and pipeline companies. In 1913, he relocated to Tulsa and became well established with several major successes in the Mid-Continent field, of which the El Dorado boom was a part. In 1916, he consolidated several smaller companies into the Sinclair Oil and Refining Company. In 1919, he established the Sinclair Consolidated Oil Corporation, a holding company with 28 subsidiaries. In the years that followed, Sinclair became one of the largest independent oil companies, with a vast network of pipelines and connections to oil facilities across the country. (The Sinclair name and dinosaur logo are registered trademarks of Sinclair Oil Corporation. All rights reserved. Used by permission.)

Deering Marshall was one of the better known local petroleum investors. Owner of a Wichita shoe store, he had owned a small plot of land with an old stone church on it. Drilling on the "Churchyard lease" in 1915, Marshall struck oil. Marshall later sold his interests to the Tidal Oil Company for $650,000. In 1918, he became president of the recently formed Kansas Oil and Gas Association.

Robert Hazlett was president of the El Dorado National Bank, and was also a major cattleman, specializing in Herefords. He helped organize both the Midland Refining Company and the Inland Oil Company. Later on, he became a major figure behind the formation of a second refinery in the area, the El Reco.

43

With towering rigs in the background, this collection of workers is busy connecting the pipes that brought oil from the wells to the rest of the world.

Three

THE BUSINESS OF OIL

From searching and pumping to refining and distribution, each step in the oil business was as much craft as science. For workers and professionals, the oil fields offered careers that paid well and had opportunities for those who were hardworking and skilled. After all, a drilling operation cost between $10,000 and $100,000, making dry holes or poor distribution systems very expensive concerns for investors. For workers, the risks were as much physical as financial. Fires, falls, and weather were just some of the dangers out on the fields. These risks added to an already competitive situation. Maps and drilling records were guarded company secrets. News of a crew striking oil was kept quiet to keep rivals from drilling nearby. Telephones operated on "party lines," forcing company officials and drilling crews to communicate in coded messages. Still, a profitable lease could launch a local company into national prominence, encouraging many firms and workers to accept the risks involved.

An area of oil exploration and development is called a field, ranging in size from a few acres to several square miles. A field may contain one lease or several. The El Dorado field alone supported over 35 leases. Oil companies usually did not outright own the land but tended to

OIL VALLEY OIL FIELDS.

lease land on which they drilled. In this image, Sinclair Oil is drilling on the Furman farm in northern Butler County.

Although initially wary of oilmen and equipment on their land, farmers and ranchers realized quickly that oil leases could supplement one's income. Arrangements usually entailed a lease on the land and a percentage of the profits if oil was found. A few farmers did very well. In 1918, one company paid $100,000 a month in royalty payments.

Knowing where to drill has always been a challenge in the oil industry. The first oil producers in Pennsylvania and Ohio studied surface landforms such as hills and streams for hints on where to drill. The practice was so tied to the geology along watercourses that it was sometimes known as "creekology." This geologist from the 1930s is exploring for enjoyment what his predecessors did for a business. (Courtesy Kansas Geological Society.)

At first, studying the structures of rock above and beneath the surface seemed little different than the educated guesses of the "creekologists." By the second decade of the 20th century, geologic surveys gradually became accepted as legitimate techniques for oil exploration. Here, C. W. Buskirk surveys landforms in early 1920.

Geologists sometimes worked as employees for the companies, while others were freelancers. The Cities Service's geology department, seen here, was one of the earliest corporate geological staffs with a training school in Bartlesville. Cities Service even had four female geologists on staff, the first in the industry.

When a site seemed promising, preliminary drilling, or "spudding," took place. This was to get a hole deep enough for the regular drilling process to take over. It was just the start of a risky and expensive operation. Nearly one out of seven wells drilled in the El Dorado field turned up dry, and many of the ones that hit oil pumped at a marginal rate at best.

It took capital to buy the equipment, hire the geologists, build the derricks and storage facilities, and pay the drilling crew. Initially, banks were wary of the boom, preferring the stability of agricultural investment. Gradually, they saw profitable investments in petroleum as well.

After spudding, the company constructed a rig to house the machinery. The most prominent feature was a tower that was usually about 50 to 60 feet high and capped with a crown block that housed pulleys for the cables. Workers constructing the rigs could make an impressive $10 a day.

The rig also housed the machinery to run the drilling operation. The apparatus in the foreground held the bit and cable. These men are on the "floor" of the rig, standing near a "bull wheel" that controlled the cables to raise and lower the bit out of the hole.

Ed Varner No. 4 Oil Well Producing 1500 Bbls Per Day
Augusta, Kans.

Powering the oil field equipment offered its own challenges. Initially, steam engines, hauled to the site by horse-drawn vehicles, provided power. Electricity and gasoline engines became more common by the 1920s. (Upper image courtesy Kansas Geological Society; lower image courtesy Wichita State University Libraries, Department of Special Collections.)

Cable tool rig drilling consisted of picking up and dropping a heavy metal bit that gradually pounded a deep hole. The bit was attached to a long cable, hence the name cable tool rig. The "walking beam," shown here, raised and lowered the cable, providing the repetitive pounding motion. Unable to see the bit, drilling crews gauged progress by monitoring the cable and how the machinery responded to the reverberating blows deep below.

Water that seeped into the hole mixed with debris and formed a sludge that had to be bailed out. A "sand wheel" on a rig operated the bailing mechanism. In addition to the drilling bits, there were tools that dressed the hole or retrieved lost equipment. (Author's collection.)

Rotary and cable tool rigs employed a wide variety of workers. For cable tool rigs, for example, a drilling crew usually had a driller who was in charge and at least one "tooldresser," or assistant whose main job was to maintain and sharpen the bits, lubricate the machinery, and run the power source. Each rig had at least two crews who worked in shifts or "tours," pronounced "towers" in oil field parlance. A driller made between $51 and $71 a week, while a tool dresser made $21 to $67. On rotary rigs, "roughnecks" helped stack and connect drill pipe, making between $15 to $30 a week.

Workers in many industries are seldom photographed. In the petroleum industry, however, both amateur and professional photographers were fond of showing workmen and the machinery they operated. Below, note the sense of humor on the sign warning of a "wild animal" at the site. The real wild animal was probably one of the workers.

The volatile Kansas weather remained a challenge for the oil industry in Butler County. In 1918, a storm in Kansas and Oklahoma destroyed several thousand rigs. On July 10, 1922, a series of tornadic winds destroyed 650 rigs in the El Dorado field alone. Many were never rebuilt.

Fire was probably the most striking and feared disaster on the fields. Concentrations of crude oil, pressurized gas, and wooden rigs made even the slightest spark a menace. Steam-powered boilers and, later on, electric motors added to the danger.

Accidents altered lives throughout the oil fields. The note on the back of this photograph reads, "This lovely lady became a widow after a marriage of only 14 days' duration as a result of the refinery fire at El Dorado, Kansas, December 29, 1918."

One of the most dangerous jobs in the field was "shooting." This involved loading nitroglycerine down the hole. The resulting explosion improved the flow of oil.

Cannons seem unlikely tools in firefighting, but firing rounds into burning tanks released oil and prevented the burning tank from exploding.

In the 1920s, the U.S. Bureau of Mines sent safety trains throughout the country to instruct oil workers about safety and first-aid techniques. Mine safety practices offered parallels to those on the oil fields. (Courtesy Wichita State University Libraries, Department of Special Collections.)

This Cities Service safety crew demonstrates their skill in handling injured comrades at a first-aid contest in Tulsa in 1932. Ben Kininkin is demonstrating artificial respiration on the "victim," August Standifer.

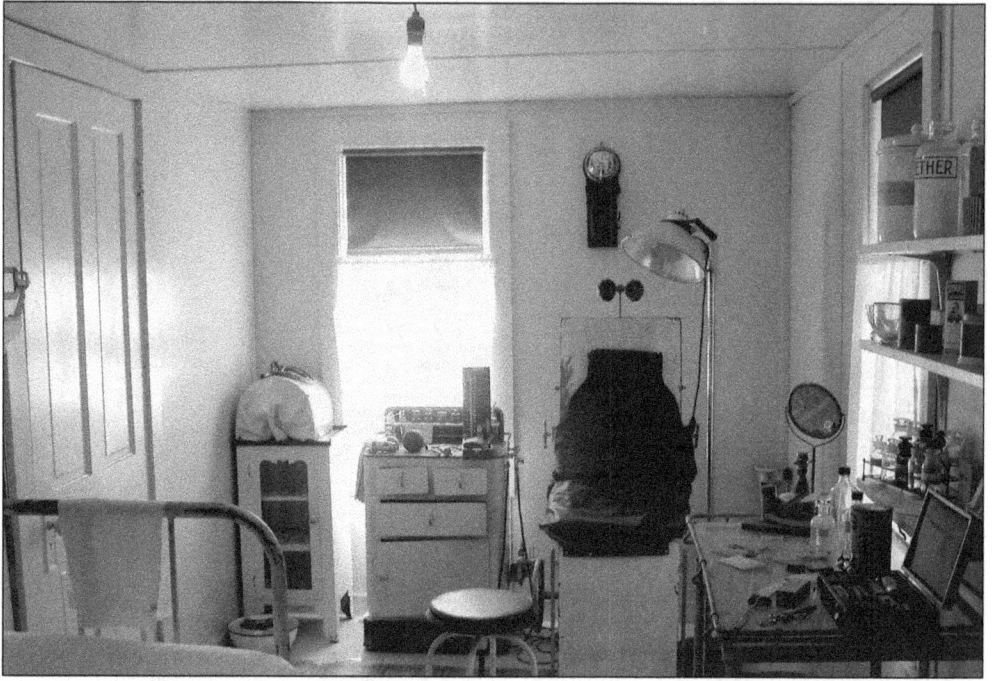

This was the era of "welfare capitalism," when providing services for employees made for a workforce that was both productive and less likely to go on strike. For example, companies provided medical care to workers. This office is a re-creation at the Kansas Oil Museum.

Office work allowed growing numbers of women opportunities in the oil fields as well. These women are in the Skelly office in El Dorado.

302

Starting in the early 20th century, the practice of drilling switched from the cable tool process to a "rotary" one, where a spinning bit at the end of a large drill pipe did the work. The rotary drill was considerably faster than the cable tool system. In just days, a rotary rig could drill holes that took a cable tool rig weeks to produce. Among the most dangerous jobs was that of derrickman, who worked high up in the derrick tower. The derrickman's job was to reach out into the rig top, where he added or removed pipe during the drilling process. Only in the 1920s did safety harnesses and railings come into widespread use. (Courtesy Wichita State University Libraries, Department of Special Collections.)

The early derricks were all wooden. Both local and national businesses specialized in their construction. As the 20th century unfolded, metal derricks became more and more common. These spindly, metal "nail derricks," in addition to being lightweight, were also more portable and more resistant to high winds. In time, the rotary process made the permanent derrick a near obsolete fixture in the oil fields. By the 1940s, the rotary drill and the metal derrick had become the standard for the industry. (Courtesy Wichita State University Libraries, Department of Special Collections.)

Something of a transition between the wooden and "nail" derrick was that of bolted metal. Augusta had several rig-building companies, including Knupp. Another company was an early developer of the nail derrick, using pipes as support elements.

Although dramatic, gushers like this one wasted thousands of barrels of oil. By the 1920s, leaders in the petroleum industry had become concerned that such activities, along with inefficient pumping and delivery systems, were hurting resources necessary for America's defense. (Lower image courtesy Augusta Historical Society.)

Most people, thanks to the movies, are familiar with the oil driller and the magnate, but when the drilling crew pulls out and the magnate returns to his movie mansion and bride, the long work begins and the long expense for the owners. A tailing-in outfit has to run tubing, rods, and a pump into the hole to lift the oil out. Storage tanks have to be set, lines laid, cement run, roads built, and a hundred other things done before the well can make a cent, and it all has to be done in a hurry. Then, if a leak develops in the tubing and the vacuum of the pump is destroyed, the tubing has to come out joint by joint until the leak is found and repaired. There is money in an oil well, money for everyone, particularly with men that keep them producing. The key to that staggering problem of production is trucks—trucks and men to drive them over roads that no car-respecting owner would set a tire on.

—James Barr, "A Success Story,"
from unpublished manuscript *Derricks*,
Wichita State University Libraries,
Department of Special Collections.

Unlike today, where each well has its own self-contained pump, oil pumping from the second decade of the 20th century through the 1920s involved several pumps connected to one power source. Some pump houses operated as many as 20 pumps. Here, a man connects pumps to the power source on the Mid Kansas Oil Company's facility on the Thrall Pool. (Courtesy Wichita State University Libraries, Department of Special Collections.)

Pumping oil required a different set of workers. Pumpers monitored the pumps and the equipment that ran them. They needed to be constantly aware of the pumps, often living right next to the equipment. Pumping workers tended to make less than the drilling crews, earning between $26 and $33 a week. "Roustabouts" maintained the equipment, were often former roughnecks from the drilling operations, and made about $5 to $7 a day.

Getting oil to storage tanks and refineries took miles and miles of pipe. This image shows the Cities Service pipeyard at its facility in Oil Hill. Over time, a network of pipelines developed akin to railroad lines, transporting oil as close as Ponca City and as far away as Chicago.

Pipe laying involved several crews of workers. Right-of-way gangs cleared brush. Stringing gangs brought the pipe to the site. Laying gangs connected the pipes and prepared the joints. Ditching gangs dug the trenches for the pipe, while covering up gangs filled in those trenches once the pipe was laid. These men are from the Prairie Pipe Line Company, an affiliate of Standard Oil.

Then as now, oil came out of the ground with lots of impurities and sediment. After being pumped, the fluid went into the bottom of the "gun barrel," where the oil floated to the top, leaving the salt water and impurities below. The oil then went into selling tanks nearby. In these images, the gun barrels are the tall, thin structures on the left. (Lower image author's collection.)

Sometimes, oil was stored in large reservoirs with earthen sides. These were usually only temporary facilities until more permanent tanks could be constructed. In addition, these ponds polluted the ground, ruined farmland, and resulted in costly cleanups.

The preference for oilmen was for wooden and metal tanks. Even so, seepage continued to be a problem. Metal tanks were also vulnerable to lightning strikes and static electricity. Thunderstorms could destroy as many as 20 tanks in the Mid-Continent field in a bad year.

The refining process for oil entailed its own set of specialized tasks. Crude oil contains a variety of hydrocarbon products, each with its own uses and boiling temperatures. At a refinery, crude oil is heated until it vaporizes. The condensed vapor is then sorted into different products. Other parts of the refinery mix, purify, and sort the different products, or fractions, by grade and use.

When crude oil is heated, the vapors rise through distillation columns. Because different hydrocarbons condense at different temperatures, the products are sorted out based on those temperatures.

Like geology, the field of chemistry made contributions to the petroleum industry. Chemists assessed the properties of refined products and developed additives that enhanced or specialized those products.

Oil and its liquid byproducts had the greatest uses at this time. Gas had a much smaller market, and the technology to ship and store it was still in its infancy. In these early years of the industry, gas produced as part of the refining process was simply flared in many cases.

Getting the finished products to market required yet another set of processes. Some products could be piped to markets. Others required special railcars. The basic structure of a tank car as a metal tube on wheels had been around since the late 1860s. Sometimes oil companies themselves owned fleets of tank cars. Sometimes, railroad companies owned the cars and charged companies a user fee.

As the motoring public became the main market for petroleum products, oil companies developed distribution systems with trucks such as these transporting gasoline to filling stations and consumers. A number of companies, including Skelly, Derby, Vickers, and Phillips, started their franchises with service stations in El Dorado and Wichita.

The petroleum industry included distribution outlets as well as drilling and refining. By the 1920s, the filling station had become a common feature on the landscape. The oil industry, conscious of its image, built stations to look like small houses that seemed appropriate for residential settings. Several companies built their first stations in southern Kansas. The first Skelly gas station, for example, was in El Dorado. This station was located at 300 North Main.

By the late 1920s, several major oil companies operated chains of stations, each with its own unique look and distinctive logo. (Author's collection.)

Companies gave their service stations standardized appearances in an attempt to foster brand awareness and loyalty on the part of the consumer. Texaco opted for a Mission Revival look. Phillips embraced the Tudor Cottage feel, a tradition that began with the first Phillips gas station that opened in Wichita in 1927. This facility is on First Street, a few blocks south of that initial Phillips station. (Courtesy Wichita-Sedgwick County Historical Museum.)

Cars, trucks, and people crowd the downtown of Oil Hill during its heyday.

Four

OIL AS A WAY OF LIFE

The El Dorado oil boom supported communities from cities to company towns. The entrepreneurs and company managers lived in the fashionable neighborhoods of Wichita and El Dorado. Heads of companies, managers, and geologists meshed with the local society, becoming pillars of many social, economic, and cultural institutions. Some employees, including office staff and refinery workers, lived in towns such as Potwin, Augusta, and El Dorado. Newly arrived oil workers and the established agricultural population sometimes existed like "oil and water" and lived in separate communities just a few miles apart.

Exact figures on the number of workers are hard to pin down because the population was so transient. Many stayed only a few months. As new opportunities emerged, families moved on to the next boom. Statistics suggest that the workforce had many Kansans but also had large numbers of people from states such as Illinois, Indiana, Missouri, Kentucky, Oklahoma, and Pennsylvania. Demographics, cultural attitudes, and company policies resulted in a workforce that was overwhelmingly white and largely native-born.

In the early years of the second decade of the 20th century, there was a small siding on the Missouri Pacific line between El Dorado and Towanda named Midian, after the Midian Shrine rite of Freemasonry. Shortly after Trapshooters No. 1 finding oil, Cities Service's extension company, the Empire Oil Company, began building a town at the site, starting with boardinghouses for single men.

Oil had hit these descendants of immigrant farmers like one of their famous cyclones and passed on leaving them richer and less happy than they'd ever been in their lives, for now they had wheat farms *and* oil, a dream *and* its fulfillment.

—James Barr, "A Success Story,"
from unpublished manuscript *Derricks*,
Wichita State University Libraries,
Department of Special Collections.

With housing scarce in El Dorado and the fields some distance away, companies often housed workers among the rigs. Some families who arrived at Midian had to make due with whatever shelter was available, from unfinished houses to converted boxcars. Some workers built their own houses out of whatever was available. When possible, workers rented homes from the company.

While pumping crews tended to be more settled and needed housing for families, drillers tended to be single and more mobile and would live in boardinghouses. Here, Jake Romesburg (left), Valley Romesburg (center), and Russell Reep are outside of Midian's boardinghouse.

The architecture of the 1800s mining boom towns reveled in ornate exuberance. Oil boom town structures, by contrast, were simple and unpretentious. Many houses were simple "shotguns," consisting of a single row of rooms. Plain wood and corrugated metal were the materials of choice. Foundations were often just timbers set on the ground. Interior walls were out of a compressed wood-chip product called beaver board. Houses varied in size, usually three to five rooms. There was running water for washing, but drinking water came from a wooden tank that went through town on a wagon. Homes did have piped-in gas, although most had outhouses in back.

Midian spread out over 28 different leases dotted with 1,132 different wells. By late 1918, Midian had a post office, a two-story railroad station, a brick school, a grocery store, a lumberyard, a bakery, a pool hall, a barbershop, a drugstore, a filling station, a baseball diamond, a community

hall for social events, and even a movie house. The "downtown" was at the intersection of Washboard Avenue (today's Shumway Road) and Silk Stocking Row—also the intersection of the Ralston, Paulson, Shumway, and Enyart leases.

Aerial View of

Oil Hill, developed shortly after Stapleton No. 1, was the other major oil town between Towanda and El Dorado. Like Midian, it was south of a Missouri-Pacific track, this time extending from El Dorado to Newton. The main buildings and offices for Cities Service oil production were along the tracks. The main town was south of the Cities Service complex. Empire Street was

the main east–west artery, complete with concrete sidewalks. Along Empire Street was a general store, a post office, a "welfare hall" (community center), filling station and garage, barbershop, and several homes designated for "foreign" workers.

Operated as divisions of the company, the towns were under the authority of company officials. These officials provided services such as medical care and rubbish removal. They also enforced order and discipline among the residents. Unruly youths could cost their fathers their jobs. In

this image from Midian, a crowd gathers at the flag raising of the infirmary. The store is on the left edge of the picture.

With workers came their children. For example, in 1915, School District 37 had closed its school in the face of declining enrollment. In early 1918, the school reopened to serve students in Midian. By 1919, it had over 500 students. Within a few years, there was a brick school, a residence for unmarried teachers, a gymnasium, and a one-story wooden high school.

Recreation was an important part of everyday life. Oil Hill had a swimming pool, tennis courts, and a small golf course.

Although El Dorado boasted that "there is not a pool room in the whole city," there were pool halls in Midian and Oil Hill. Kansas had been a "dry" state since the 1880s, but roadhouses and other establishments did provide alcohol. Those wanting the diversions of a larger city could go to dances, movies, and clubs in El Dorado or Wichita.

Smaller oil communities existed throughout Butler County. In the southern part of the county, the Tidal Oil Company operated in Magna City, east of Douglass on the Fox-Bush Pool. The long, low building is the hotel. O. V. Jewell's store is on the right.

The field between Gordon and Augusta supported Haskin's Camp (shown here), Browntown, Pine Oil Camp, and Reeve's Lease. Some "oil camps" were not official towns but simply collections of homes near the rigs.

Oil Valley, Kans.

The main oil community in northern Butler County was Oil Valley, east of Elbing. Developed in response to strikes on the Leydig and Lathrop farms, the community had its own stores and entertainment venues—as well as a branch bank and a post office. Even after the post office closed in 1922, workers continued living in the Oil Valley area into the 1930s.

Oil also changed the lives of people in established towns such as Augusta and El Dorado. Oil companies often had their offices—or branch offices in the case of the larger firms—in these towns.

This scene shows the interior of the Parkersburg Rig and Reel Supply on North Vine in El Dorado. L. F. Mulhusen is on the left, and T. H. Davis is on the right.

Office of the Empire Gas and Fuel Co. Oil Hill Ks.

Butler County's population had nearly doubled from over 23,000 in 1910 to over 43,000 in 1920. Much of this growth took place in communities like Midian and Oil Hill, to the disdain of some El Doradans. One Oil Hiller recalled, "There was some mighty fancy nose lifting and . . . many El Dorado ladies somehow got the idea that the good Lord made them a bit better'n ours."

The Arkansas Valley Interurban system was developed in the second decade of the 20th century to connect Wichita with towns in south-central Kansas. As early as 1917, the company looked into extending lines to El Dorado and the oil communities. However, the war effort's demand for materials and money doomed plans for this "Walnut Valley Interurban." By the 1920s, improved road connections allowed cars and trucks to handle local traffic. (Courtesy Wichita State University Libraries, Department of Special Collections.)

Even so, roads were still challenging. Most were unpaved, turning to "gumbo" when it rained.

Baseball was the dominant sport of the age. Towns and companies fielded their own teams.

Companies were still small enough to hold annual picnics for their employees. Derby's 1923 picnic, for example, hosted over 400 workers and their families, complete with a parade in Wichita. This image shows the Skelly employee picnic of 1927.

Emerging as a national movement in the early 20th century, the Ku Klux Klan had a presence in Butler County. Pioneer Klan No. 1, in El Dorado, reported membership of 4,000 in 1918. With few African Americans in the region, the Klan in Augusta targeted what it perceived as rowdiness on the part of some of the oil workers.

Antilabor sentiments and a transient workforce limited attempts to unionize oil workers. In addition, many workers not satisfied with wages or conditions could choose among several other companies for employment. Organizations such as the Oil Workers International Union did make some inroads such as among the relatively settled refinery workers, as this parade in Augusta shows. (Courtesy Augusta Historical Society.)

Local businesses did well with oil companies and their workers nearby. Even the businesses had to adapt to longer hours. Derricks operated 24 hours a day with crews working in shifts, or "tours." For those in the night tour, drugstores and other establishments were open at night as well as during the day.

More than just reporters of news, newspaper editors were also influential local leaders and community promoters. In El Dorado, that figure was Rolla A. Clymer, who got his start working for the respected *Emporia Gazette* of William Allen White. Clymer came to El Dorado in 1918, taking on the editorship of the *Republican* (a paper for which White himself had once been a reporter).

Several oil companies had their offices in Wichita, often along Lawrence Avenue (now Broadway). Built in 1929, the Ellis-Singleton building housed the offices of nearly a dozen oil companies and geology firms. In 1942, to reflect its tenants, the structure officially became the Petroleum Building. (Author's collection.)

Warren Brown, once mayor of Augusta, also invested in oil, with leases very close to the original Varner strike. By the early 1920s, he had enough money to build this fashionable house in the College Hill neighborhood. When he died in 1956, Brown was reported to have been the richest man in Kansas. (Author's collection.)

In 1923, a group of geologists met at Wichita's Innes Tea Room and formed what eventually became the Kansas Geological Society. The society's main service has been to maintain the Kansas Well Log Bureau, collecting the drilling logs of oil and gas tests throughout the state, pooling what had been the possessions of individual companies. The organization also hosted field trips, such as this one in 1930, to New Mexico. (Courtesy Kansas Geological Society.)

In the 1920s, real estate developer Alton Smith planned an exclusive residential community about a mile east of Wichita called Eastborough Estates. In 1930, things changed when oil was discovered on the site. Efforts of E. B. Shawver, the E. W. Marland Company of Oklahoma, and others resulted in several wells on the Eastborough Pool. Today, Eastborough is its own city, now completely surrounded by Wichita. (Author's collection.)

A flare and refinery can be seen in the distance of this nighttime view.

Five

THE LEGACY CONTINUES

Oil seemed like the miracle fuel, liberating society from coal-fired boilers and horse-drawn vehicles. Automobiles and aircraft suggested a future of clean and efficient travel. In Kansas, success in El Dorado inspired exploration in the central and western parts of the state. The discovery of oil fields in places like Russell and Hugoton shifted the focus of the Kansas oil industry, while entrepreneurs in Wichita focused their attention on new ventures such as aviation. By the 1930s, production in the El Dorado oil field slowed to a more modest level as remaining companies and workers concentrated on other opportunities. Towns like those of Midian and Oil Hill shrank and vanished even as the refineries in El Dorado modernized and expanded. Today, the legacy of the Butler County oil boom lives on in the legion of pumps still dotting the landscape, in the aircraft that fly overhead, and in El Dorado's Kansas Oil Museum.

Iryl W. Murfin grew up in Missouri and arrived in El Dorado as a tool dresser. In the 1920s, he formed his own drilling company and continued in that business until 1963. The Murfin Drilling Company grew from its base in the El Dorado field, one of several companies that specialized in drilling. Murfin's sons, William R. and Fred, took over management of the company in the years that followed. Murfin's grandson David L. became president of the company in 1992.

In Reno County, the oil and salt industries shared a common geology and history. In 1887, Ben Blanchard discovered salt while drilling for oil, sparking a boom in salt. This image is of the facility for Carey Salt, opened in 1922 as one of the first salt mines in the area (earlier plants processed salt brine). In the 1920s, oil exploration again resumed in the county, part of an expansion of oil drilling in central Kansas. (Author's collection.)

In 1923, Ed Oswald and his wife, Carrie, were in danger of losing their Russell County ranch. The Oswalds agreed to have the M. M. Valerius Oil Company drill on a lease that Carrie Oswald had. On Thanksgiving Day, November 23, drilling crews brought up oil at what became Carrie Oswald No. 1, shown here, transforming Russell into the state's next oil town. (Courtesy Kansas Oil and Gas Hall of Fame and Museum.)

Oil exploration in southwestern Kansas took off in Seward County in the wake of the success of Crawford No. 1 near Hugoton in 1927. In the years that followed, Hugoton and western Kansas became the state's main region for both oil and gas production. (Courtesy Wichita State University Libraries, Department of Special Collections.)

In the 1920s and 1930s, oil companies such as Cities Service developed the practice of "secondary recovery"—injecting air and water into existing wells to increase pressure and output. This facility is from one of the first such projects in Butler County, focusing particularly upon the shoestring pools. Sometimes, the pressure forced oil out of long forgotten, unplugged holes, causing oil and brine to ooze across the surface.

Harry Gore was a Jewish immigrant who initially became a drilling contractor in Ohio. In 1916, he came to the El Dorado fields and played a major role in the discovery of the Smock-Sluss pool. By the time of his death in 1951, he had drilled over 1,500 wells in Kansas and throughout the Southwest.

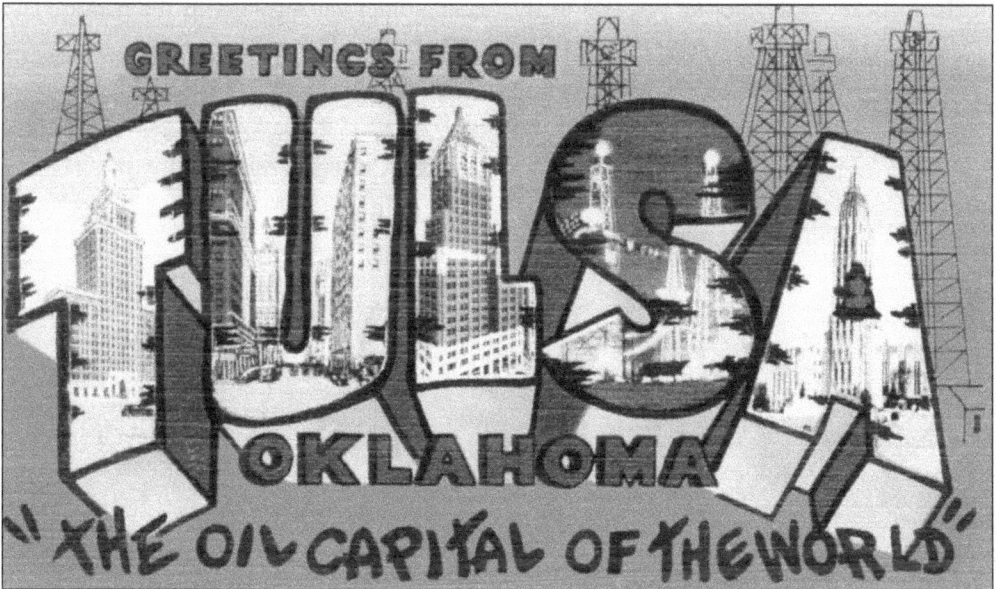

GREETINGS FROM TULSA OKLAHOMA "THE OIL CAPITAL OF THE WORLD"

Oklahoma continued to surge as one of the leading oil-producing states, pumping out double the barrels of Kansas. Much of this production was in Oklahoma, where companies such as Marland developed pools in places such as Tonkawa. Meanwhile, Tulsa positioned itself firmly as the oil capital of the region, becoming the headquarters for American Association of Petroleum Geologists as well as several oil companies. (Author's collection; used with permission of the Lake County Discovery Museum.)

In the early 1900s, California emerged as the leading oil-producing state in the nation. The Santa Fe Springs field near Los Angeles was just one of many important oil centers. (Author's collection; used with permission of the Lake County Discovery Museum.)

By 1919, Texas had established itself as the third major oil-producing state of the country. Development occurred in two main areas. One was along the coast in places such as the Spindletop field, shown here. The other major concentration was in west Texas, with places like Odessa and Amarillo becoming oil centers in their own right. (Author's collection; used with permission of the Lake County Discovery Museum.)

Oil prices rose to over $3 a barrel in 1920. By 1923, it was on average about $1.45. Companies nationwide found themselves having to cut back, and in response, banks had to write off loans to oil companies. Production in Butler County also declined from the wartime high of over 36 million barrels to just over 5 million in 1926. (Courtesy Kansas Oil and Gas Hall of Fame and Museum.)

As oil development moved to central and western Kansas, the workers went with it. In Butler County, the first major layoffs began between 1921 and 1922. By 1930, Butler County had lost 18 percent of its 1920 population of over 8,000 people. By contrast, in western and central Kansas, newly arrived families found themselves living near the same neighbors they had in Butler County.

108

While farmers welcomed the revenue that oil wells brought, leaky pipes, unplugged drill holes, and leaking tanks spread oil and salt water across fields. Oil drilling and production has also impacted water resources, both groundwater and flowing streams. While oil companies and investors received the financial benefits of production, the cost of cleaning up afterward often fell on local landowners, who, in turn, demanded action on the part of the oil company. If a company refused, a lawsuit might be brought up to enforce matters. Occasionally, the taxpayers ended up bearing the costs of the cleanup. (Courtesy Wichita-Sedgwick County Historical Museum.)

Kansas has had a long association with the motorcar. One of the most famous Kansans in automotive history was Walter P. Chrysler. Born in Wamego, Chrysler grew up in Ellis in north-central Kansas. Walter's father was an engineer for the Union Pacific, and in time Walter too worked for that railroad. Soon, however, his interest turned to the automobile. He started working for the Buick Motor Company in the second decade of the 20th century and eventually became the firm's president. In the early 1920s, Chrysler went on to transform ailing companies such as Willys-Overland and Maxwell into profitable ventures. Chrysler formed his own automobile company in 1925 and served as its president until 1935. He remained an active part of the company until his death in 1940. Chrysler's boyhood home still stands as a museum on Highway 40. (Author's collection.)

In the early 20th century, local businessman Woody Hockaday helped motorists navigate the complicated jumble of local roads in the years before interstate highways. Following his maps and H signs that dotted the landscape, travelers could make their way across the prairies. Later in life, Hockaday became better known for his eccentricities than his pioneering roadwork. (Courtesy Wichita-Sedgwick County Historical Museum.)

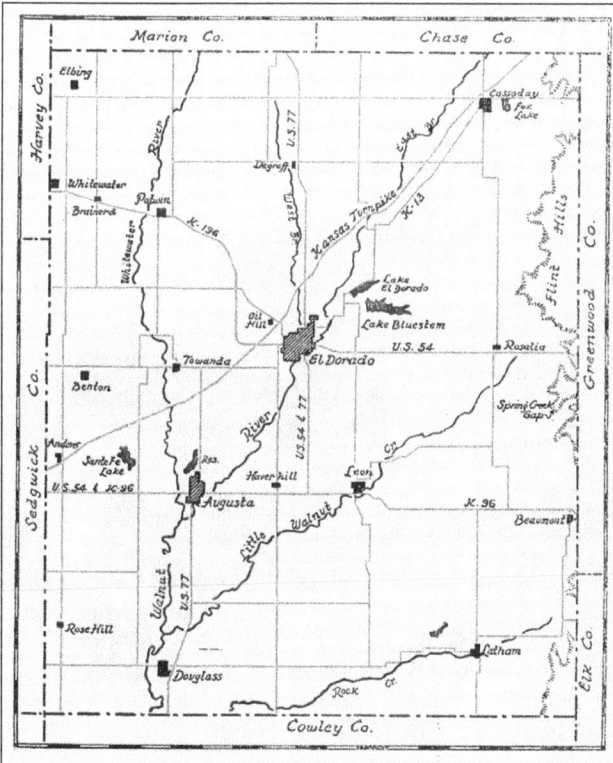

In the decades that followed, a network of federally coordinated highways connected the country. Highway 50, one of the main east–west routes, ran about 35 miles north of the El Dorado field. Highway 54 (also known as the Cannonball Highway) ran across the lower third of Kansas, right through El Dorado. This postcard from the Walnut Valley State Bank shows these roads.

111

Jacob Melvin Moellendick, shown here on the left next to his son, was an oilman who has the reputation of being the father of aviation in Wichita. It was Jacob Moellendick who, with a team of investors, brought to Wichita aviation pioneers E. M. "Matty" Laird and George "Buck" Weaver to form the Laird Aircraft Company in 1919. The company became the Swallow Aircraft Company in the early 1920s. (Courtesy Kansas Aviation Museum.)

The Laird Aircraft Company brought in other aviation pioneers, including Walter Beech and Lloyd Stearman. Moellendick's prickly personality did not sit well with the fliers, and differences of opinion soon emerged. By early 1925, Stearman and Beech left and joined with Clyde Cessna to form their own company, Travel Air. During the Great Depression, Travel Air foundered, but Cessna, Beech, and Stearman remained important parts of the community. (Courtesy Kansas Aviation Museum.)

As with automobile racing today, companies sponsored racers and planes, sometimes to test and promote their own lines of aviation fuels. Travel Air built "mystery ships" that sported the colors and liveries of at least two oil companies, Shell and Texaco. Meanwhile, Frank Phillips sponsored another Wichita-built Travel Air airplane, the *Woolaroc*, which won the 1927 Dole Race to Hawaii. Art Goebel (in the knickers) was the *Woolaroc*'s pilot. (Courtesy Wichita State University Libraries, Department of Special Collections.)

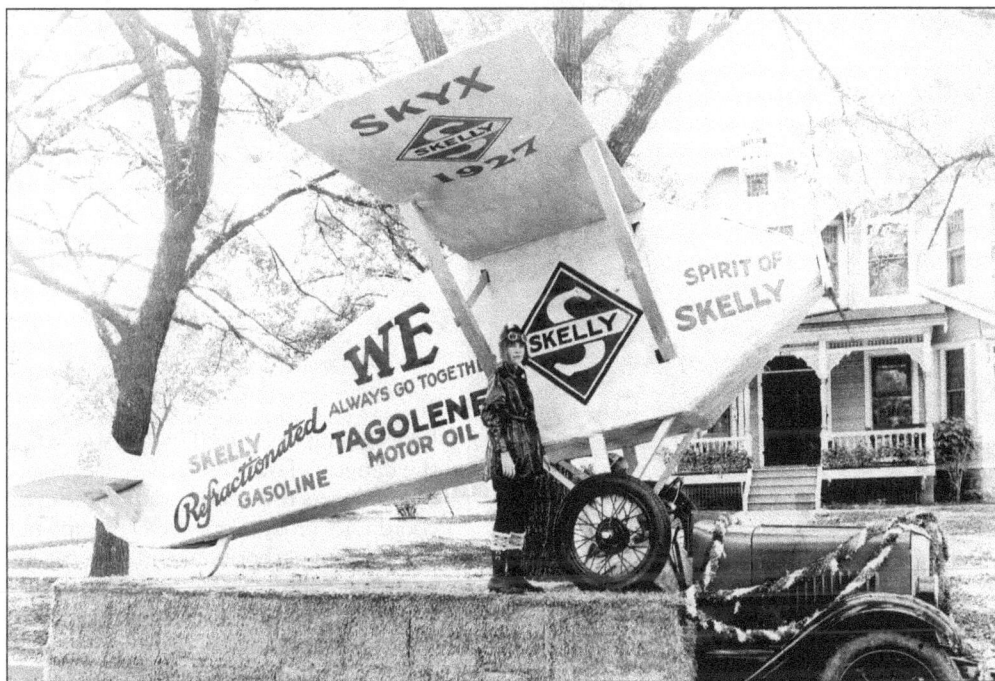

Like Jake Moellendick, William Skelly invested in aviation as well, founding Tulsa's Spartan Aircraft Company and Southwest Air Fast Express. This promotional float, dating from 1927, was patterned after Charles Lindbergh's famous *Spirit of St. Louis*.

Although the Great Depression and Dust Bowl devastated Kansas in the 1930s, the oil industry enabled some communities to ride out the decade. The main concentration of oil production had shifted to the center part of the state, but there were still 2,701 producing wells in Butler County in 1934.

Like agriculture, the oil industry faced the dangers of overproduction. Regional oil producers responded by attempting to coordinate production, even bringing in government authority to curb companies from flooding the market. Among these supporters was Alf Landon, governor of Kansas, who encouraged the passage of legislation that regulated both pipelines and production. In 1936, Landon went on to be a presidential candidate against Franklin Roosevelt.

Ernest B. Shawver was a key figure in the movement to better plan oil production in Kansas. Getting his start in the 1920s, Shawver helped develop the Eastborough Pool. A few years later, he was among the founding members of an organization of local producers that became the Kansas Independent Oil and Gas Association (KIOGA).

Originally from Texas, Fred C. Koch was among the innovators of refining. He, P. C. Keith, and Lewis Winkler formed their own engineering company. In the 1930s, the work even extended into the Soviet Union. After World War II, Koch formed his own company that expanded beyond refining to include pipelines, chemicals, and even ranching.

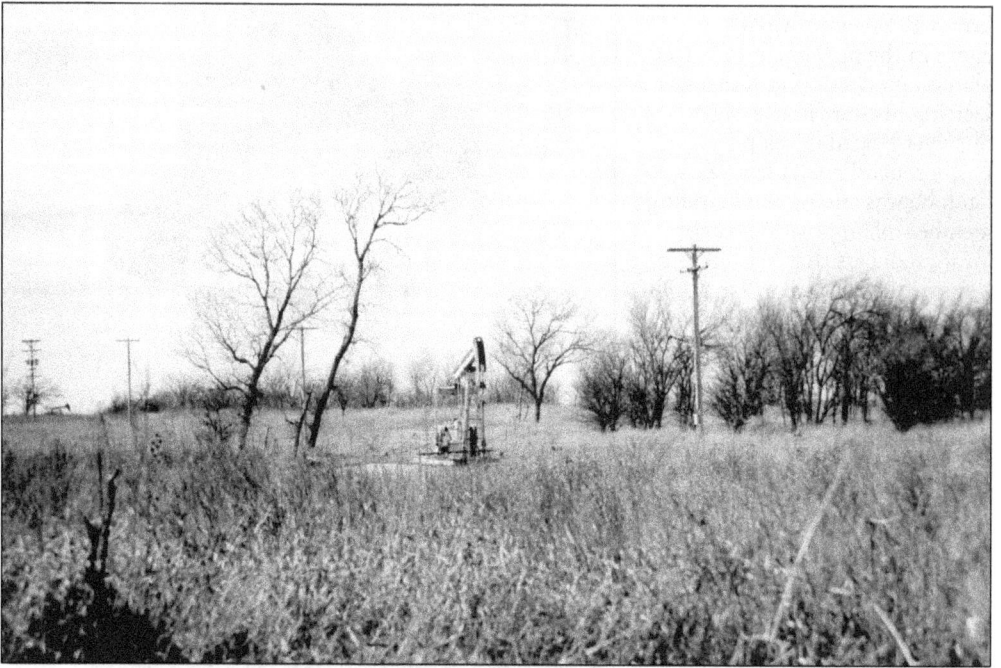

Communities such as Midian and Oil Hill existed to support companies such as Cities Service. When Cities Service decided to concentrate its resources in other areas, the company no longer needed to maintain these communities. Midian was the first to go, declining gradually as workers were laid off or moved elsewhere. Cities Service tore down the vacant structures or sold them on the condition that they were moved somewhere else. Many became homes or outbuildings for people throughout the county. In 1940, the school closed. With the loss of the school, Midian quickly declined. In 1950, its post office closed. In the decades that followed, the original landowners requested the company clear away as much remaining debris as possible. Today the largest remaining structure is the power plant. (Author's collection.)

Oil Hill declined a little more slowly. Its major changes took place about a decade after those of Midian. Rows of tidy homes continued into the late 1940s, even while family after family moved out or relocated. In the late 1950s, construction of the new Highway 196 bypassed the community. In 1958, Cities Service moved those who were left, closed the town for good, and tore down most of the structures. Ralph and Marion Moulton's cafe remained until May 1969. Today only a few battered metal buildings and bits of concrete sidewalk poke out among the now overgrown trees and bushes that once marked the front and back yards of Oil Hill's homes.

World War II and the postwar boom brought a brief revival of oil development in the El Dorado area. Kansas's oil production peaked in 1956, with over 1,800 wells in Butler County alone. Oil and the industries it supported continued to bring prosperity to places such as El Dorado and Wichita, whose Douglas Avenue appears here at dusk in 1959. (Courtesy Les Broadstreet.)

The region continued to be a center for refining. El Reco, Skelly, and the other refineries expanded and modernized in the 1940s and 1950s. El Reco eventually became part of the American Petrofina Company before it closed in the mid-1980s. The Skelly refinery became part of Getty, then Texaco, and currently Frontier. Today it is the largest refinery in Kansas.

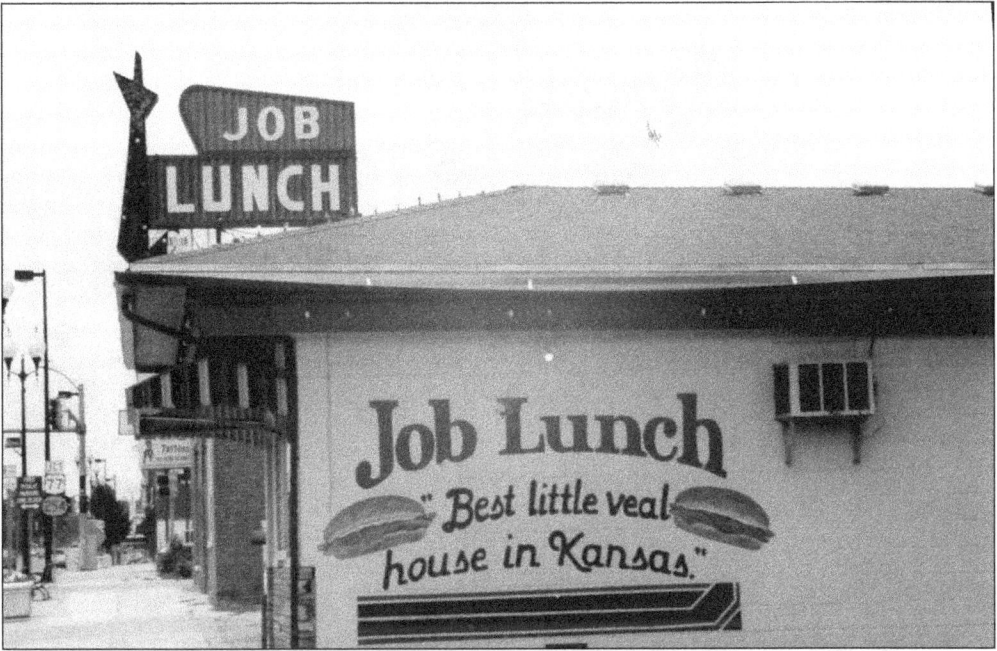

Restaurants and cafes developed to feed locals and travelers alike. Job Lunch, the "Best Little Veal House in Kansas," is on the main east–west street in El Dorado, part of Highway 54. (Author's collection.)

In 1949, a group of over 300 oil professionals chartered the Petroleum Club in Wichita. Kansas had recently repealed its ban on alcohol but only allowed liquor by the glass to be served in private clubs, encouraging their development in the 1940s and 1950s. Initially restricted only to members of the oil and gas industries, the Petroleum Club became an important social center for leaders in the oil community.

By the 1950s, the individual pump jack eclipsed the pump house arrangement for getting oil out of wells. Over time, the bobbing, dinosaur-like machines replaced the derrick as the main symbol of the industry. (Upper image author's collection; lower image courtesy Pickrell Drilling Company.)

The efforts of another Kansan, Pres. Dwight Eisenhower, spelled major changes for the region. As it developed, the interstate system absorbed the already constructed Kansas Turnpike, as part of Interstate 35. The turnpike's route cut diagonally across Butler County, with the sites of Oil Hill and Midian on one side and El Dorado on the other.

In 1928, El Doradans dedicated Lake El Dorado, a small reservoir east of town, as a water supply. Just to the north was Lake Bluestem. In the 1970s, the Tulsa District of the Army Corps of Engineers connected the two bodies into an even larger reservoir (El Dorado Lake) for flood control and improved recreational opportunities.

WHITE EAGLE REFINERY, AUGUSTA, KANSAS
Capacity 10,000 Barrels of Crude Oil Per Day

In the early 1930s, the White Eagle Refinery became part of the Standard Oil Company of New York (Socony), a firm that later transformed itself into Mobil Oil. By the 1980s, its value to the company had diminished, and the refinery was shut down in 1984. With this major employer gone, Augusta has looked for new sources of income and identity. (Courtesy Wichita State University Libraries, Department of Special Collections.)

In recent years, economic trends and government policies have favored the expansion of large refineries at the expense of smaller ones. In the 1970s, Derby became part of the Coastal Corporation. In Wichita, the Derby refinery remained active into the 1990s. After it closed, the refinery itself was demolished as part of a revitalization along 21st Street. (Author's collection.)

As the oil industry in Kansas changed, El Doradans began to take an interest in their local history. In 1940, citizens marked the Stapleton No. 1 with this monument, long before the well stopped production in 1967.

Clifford W. Stone was one of a number of people who worked to preserve and promote the region's history. Stone served as a farms manager, as CEO of Walnut Valley Bank and Trust, and as managing director of Saco and Yuma oil companies for many years. He was also active in establishing the Butler County Historical Society, the Kansas Oil Museum, and the Kansas Oil and Gas Legacy Hall of Fame.

In 1956, several El Doradans, including Rolla Clymer and Clifford Stone, incorporated the Butler County Historical Society. After occupying a number of local buildings, the organization moved into its current structure in 1976. Here, Charles Heilman (left), Clifford W. Stone (center), and Clay Riley cut the ribbon at the opening ceremony. Today, the society shares that space with the Kansas Oil Museum and Kansas Oil and Gas Legacy Gallery.

While the main focus is on the oil industry, Butler County's agricultural heritage is also on display at the museum. (Author's collection.)

Over the 20th century, the United States became dependent on foreign oil, especially from the Middle East. By the 1970s, the country realized how vulnerable it was. Gas shortages resulted in high prices and long lines as people queued to fill up their cars. This scene from California was repeated nationwide. (Courtesy Theodore C. Price.)

Today, Kansas remains a major oil-producing state. Even so, companies and drillers continue to have to balance the cost of exploration and development with expected gains. As in the second decade of the 20th century, heavy investment in drilling might produce a new gusher or a very expensive dry hole in the ground. (Courtesy Pickrell Drilling Company.)

As energy needs continue to develop, there has been growing interest in wind technology. Some feel that this wind farm in Gray County represents the future, and they call for similar structures in the El Dorado area. Others are concerned that rows of wind generators would ruin the Flint Hills. As ever, risks, opportunity, and debate shape the land and the people of the El Dorado field. (Author's collection.)

I dreamed that the good old oil days were over forever more,
And that I had just arrived upon that golden shore.
Of oil men there I saw a few,
Of railroaders there were just two.

—Anonymous,
from collection of Roxie Olmstead.

BIBLIOGRAPHY

Dorsey, Hagen. *Oil Field Practice*. New York: McGraw-Hill Book Company, 1921.

Ellis, William Donohue. *On the Oil Lands with Cities Service*. Tulsa, OK: Cities Service Oil and Gas Company, 1983.

Fath, A. G. *Geology of the Eldorado Oil and Gas Field, Butler County, Kansas*. State Geological Survey of Kansas Bulletin 7. Lawrence, KS: State Geological Survey of Kansas, 1921.

Fisher, R. H. *Biographical Sketches of El Dorado Citizens*. El Dorado, KS: Thompson Brothers Stationary & Printing Company, 1930.

Green, William Allen. *Midian: Kansas History of an Oil Boom Town*. Wichita, KS: Copycat Service Company, 1964.

Klintworth, Lawrence P., ed. *The Kingdom of Butler*. El Dorado, KS: Butler County Historical Society, 1980.

Moore, Raymond C., and Winthrop Haynes. *Oil and Gas Resources in Kansas*. State Geological Survey of Kansas Bulletin 3. Lawrence, KS: State Geological Survey of Kansas, 1917.

King, Marsha. *Results of Phase III Archeological Investigations at the Midian Townsite 14BU381, Butler County, Kansas*. Contract Archaeology Publication No. 13. Topeka, KS: Kansas State Historical Society, 1996.

Klintworth, Lawrence P. *Oil Hill: The Town That Cities Service Built*. El Dorado, KS: Butler County Historical Society, 1977.

Miner, Craig. *Discovery!: Cycles of Change in the Kansas Oil and Gas Industry 1860–1987*. Wichita, KS: Kansas Independent Oil and Gas Association, 1987.

———. *The Fire in the Rock: A History of the Oil and Gas Industry in Kansas 1855–1976*. Wichita, KS: Kansas Independent Oil and Gas Association, 1976.

Nessly, M. E., ed. *Illustrated Directory of Kansas Oil Men with Their Commercial Interests and Homes*. Reprint of original 1918 by Municipal Publicity Company. El Dorado, KS: Butler County Historical Society.

Reddish, Sandra. "The Unobtrusive Soldier: Corporal Harry Gilmore, 1917–1919." Master's thesis, Wichita State University, 2003.

Schruben, Francis W. *Wea Creek to El Dorado: OIL in Kansas, 1860–1920*. Columbia, MO: University of Missouri Press, 1972.

Stratford, Perry Jessie. *Butler County's Eighty Years: 1855–1935*. El Dorado, KS: Butler County News, 1934.

www.ingramcontent.com/pod-product-compliance
Lightning Source LLC
Chambersburg PA
CBHW080626110426
42813CB00006B/1609